Wreck Diver
Manual

Improve Your Scuba

PADI®

Wreck Diver
Manual

Published by PADI
30151 Tomas Street
Rancho Santa Margarita, CA 92688-2125

Library of Congress Card Number 95-071223
ISBN 1-878663-20-8

Printed in the United States of America
10 9 8 7 6 5 4 3

PRODUCT NO. 79304 (Rev. 6/03) Version 1.3

Table of Contents

Introduction

As you descend, you look below for your first glimpse. Your eyes instinctively search for pattern — something that looks like a ship. You near the bottom and suddenly, in a blink, the wreck materializes below you.

Whether your first or your hundredth dive on it, few moments in diving compare with descending on a wreck. The first few times, you sense the mystery and exhilaration of discovery. Once you get to know it, each dive rings with familiarity, reminding you of the last time you visited. In some environments, you see changes from one dive to the next as the wreck gradually evolves from a work of humanity to part of the underwater world. In other environments, the wreck seems timeless — you age and change over the years, but it doesn't.

While most people think "ship" when they think of a wreck, wreck diving includes other craft, such as sail boats, houseboats, railroad cars, automobiles, aircraft and military craft. Because of this, few dive environments lack wrecks, so virtually every diver ends up diving on wrecks from time to time. Nonetheless, boats and ships do make up the majority of wrecks, so the references you'll read in this manual apply primarily to them.

The PADI Wreck Diver Specialty course teaches the basic principles for fun, safe wreck diving. The course was designed for flexibility, so that what you learn applies when diving on both very intact wrecks, and wrecks that have become little more than a rubble pile. Whether wrecks interest you out of historical curiosity or because they're artificial reefs with abundant life, this program will help you enjoy wreck diving more and help you avoid potential problems.

Course Overview

The PADI Wreck Diver program is divided into knowledge development and open water training. The knowledge development portion explains the principles and information you need for making and enjoying recreational wreck dives, with topics including wreck diving law, hazards to avoid, how to research wrecks, and the basics of wreck penetration. Knowledge development is usually handled through independent study with this manual (see "How to Use This Book") and the PADI *Wreck Diving* video (see "Getting the Most from the PADI *Wreck Diving* video), and review sessions prior to open water training. At his discretion, your instructor may schedule more formal classroom sessions.

During open water training, you'll apply the knowledge you've learned as you develop wreck diving skills. As you master these techniques, you'll learn to adapt what you practice to suit the wreck you're diving on and your personal interests. You'll

The PADI Adventure Diver or PADI Advanced Open Water Program is a prerequisite for the Wreck Diver Course; the PADI Deep Diver course is also recommended if you'll be exploring wrecks deeper than 18 metres/60 feet.

practice these skills on a wreck during at least four wreck dives, though your instructor may add additional dives and/or confined water (pool) sessions at his discretion, based on the local diving environment, and on your needs and interests.

PADI Wreck Diver Certification Prerequisites

To enroll in the PADI Wreck Diver course, you must be certified as a PADI Adventure Diver or PADI Advanced Open Water Diver or have a qualifying certification similar to that of a PADI Advanced Open Water Diver from another organization.

If you'll be diving on wrecks deeper than 18 metres/ 60 feet, it's also recommended (but not required) that you successfully complete the PADI Deep Diver course. This course develops knowledge and skills appropriate for diving to an absolute maximum depth of 40 metres/ 130 feet.

How to Use This Book

The PADI *Wreck Diver Manual* is an interactive book that assists you in learning the material you read. The following guidelines will help you maximize your learning:

First, find a quiet, comfortable place to study without distractions. Then, begin by previewing the section you're going to read by skimming through it, reading italicized or boldfaced words, and subheadings and captions. After previewing, return to the beginning of the section.

You'll notice that each section has a set of Study Objectives stated as questions. Read these before beginning to read each section. Now, look for the answers as you read, underlining or highlighting them as you find them. When you finish reading the section, review your underlined/highlit answers.

At the end of each section, you'll find a short exercise that assesses your comprehension. Answer

Getting the Most from the PADI Wreck Diving Video

The companion video to this program is the PADI *Wreck Diving* video, which shows you the wreck diving techniques you'll read about here and practice with your PADI Instructor. Studying with the video enhances learning because you'll see role model demonstrations of techniques, with emphasis on important skills. You can also slow down, rewind and rewatch sections as necessary.

You'll find the *Wreck Diving* video speeds learning whether you watch it first, then read this manual, or vice versa. The following method represents an optimum study method, but people differ in how they learn. As long as you integrate manual and video study, use the approach that suits you best:

Begin by watching the *Wreck Diving* video in a comfortable area. The idea is to get an overview of what you'll be learning, both in this manual and during your open water sessions.

Next, read this manual as directed by your instructor. Be sure to highlight/underline study objective material, answer the exercises and complete the Knowledge

Review. As you do so, you'll recognize the principles and philosophies behind the techniques you saw in the video, with some of the detail now enhanced.

Before each open water training session, rewatch the corresponding portion of the video. After reading the manual, you'll comprehend more detail from what you see, and what you've learned will be refreshed and reinforced. This best prepares you for each Wreck Training dive.

Finally, rewatch the PADI *Wreck Diving* video periodically after you've completed the course. This is an effective way to keep your wreck diving knowledge refreshed, and a good review prior to practicing wreck diving techniques to keep them current.

each question by marking directly in your book, then compare it with the correct answer provided. If you miss a question, reread the relevant material until you understand what you missed.

At the end of the manual, you'll find a Knowledge Review. Your instructor will have you complete the Knowledge Review for review. By the time you complete the Knowledge Review, you should be familiar with the material. However, if there's something you don't understand despite rereading the material, be sure to have your instructor explain it to you.

Important

While you can learn many aspects of wreck diving by reading the PADI *Wreck Diver Manual* and by watching the PADI *Wreck Diving* video, nothing replaces actual training from a qualified PADI Instructor. This is especially true if you're interested in wreck penetration. Practicing penetration techniques without the proper supervision can create hazardous situations. See your local PADI Instructor, Dive Center or Resort if you have not yet enrolled in a PADI Wreck Diver course.

Note to student: For clarity, some photographs in this book show a single diver. Remember, however, that somebody — the diver's buddy — was there to *take* the picture. Therefore, this doesn't imply that the buddy system can be disregarded.

Watch for These Symbols

 Alerts you to important safety information. Pay close attention when you see this symbol and consult your instructor if you do not understand the material.

 This Project A.W.A.R.E. symbol highlights information and techniques that allow you to harmoniously interact with the aquatic environment.

 Alerts you to additional/related information available on PADI videos.

 Alerts you to additional sources of deeper and/or broader topic coverage. This symbol is for your interest and further reading; all information necessary for the PADI Wreck Diver course is in this manual.

PADI Specialty Diver Course and Advanced Open Water Program Relationship

Each Adventure Dive of the PADI Adventures in Diving program is the first dive from a corresponding PADI Specialty Diver course. If taking the Wreck Adventure Dive as one of your elective dives for certification as an Adventure Diver or Advanced Open Water Diver, you may credit the Wreck Adventure Dive as Dive One of the Wreck Diver Specialty.

PADI Specialties with corresponding Adventure Dives include: Altitude, AWARE – Fish Identification, Boat Diver, Deep Diver, Diver Propulsion Vehicle Diver, Drift Diver, Dry Suit Diver, Multilevel Diver, Night Diver, Peak Performance Buoyancy, Search and Recovery Diver, Underwater Naturalist, Underwater Navigator, Underwater Photographer, Underwater Videographer and Wreck Diver.

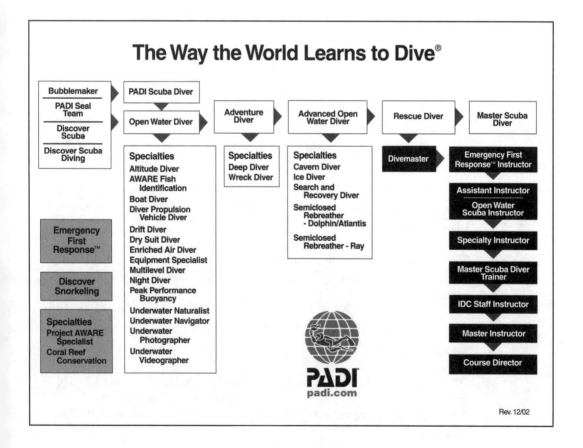

The Way the World Learns to Dive®

Rev. 12/02

Study Objectives

Underline/highlight the answers to these questions as you read:

1. What are four common reasons why people wreck dive?

The Appeal of Wreck Diving

People differ in their interests when it comes to wreck diving. It's possible to find yourself diving with someone who has the same excitement about the dive as you, but for a completely different reason. Like deep diving, night diving and other dive specialties, you may find dozens of reasons why wreck diving interests various divers. You and your future dive partners may get more out of wreck diving if you recognize how it appeals to different people.

Curiosity

Wrecks fascinate many divers. You may find yourself curious about what's inside them, what sank them and what they were like before they went down. You may find this curiosity manifests itself through adventure: the challenge of exploring wrecks and a glimpse into the unknown.

History

Some divers see wrecks as time capsules holding clues to mankind's past. Wrecks may interest you as tangible historical and archaeological resources that tell us something about who we once were, and what we once did.

You may find yourself interested in wrecks out of curiosity, or because they're tangible historical resources.

Aquatic life

In most underwater environments, a sunken ship quickly attracts aquatic life, slowly transforming into an artificial reef. Even in freshwater sites where aquatic life isn't as conspicuous or varied as in the ocean, wrecks attract fish and other organisms.

Many divers find wrecks interesting dive sites because they're artifical reefs teeming with life.

1

Wreck Diving World Hot Spots: Truk Lagoon

Of all the top wreck diving spots around the world, one of the most famous is Truk Lagoon, with its dozens of coral encrusted World War II shipwrecks. Truk Lagoon lies just above the equator in the Pacific in Micronesia, northeast of Papau New Guinea.

On February 17, 1944, Allied aircraft caught the Japanese Combined Fleet at anchor in the lagoon, beginning an attack that eventually involved 450 aircraft. In two days, more than 50 ships were sunk or sinking.

Today more than a dozen wrecks lie within reach of recreational divers. Some are so shallow you can snorkel on them, while others begin at moderate depths and reach beyond the limits of recreational diving. Resting in warm water, these wrecks are spectacular, both as wrecks and as living coral reefs. Divers may visit the wrecks, but it's illegal to remove or disturb anything.

You may be interested in a wreck more for its role as a reef than as an artifact or challenge. Wrecks provide something unique for those interested in underwater natural history — a reef with a known (or approximate) date of origin. This makes it possible to estimate how fast some types of organisms spread and grow. In some areas, wrecks may be the only dive sites with appreciable concentrations of aquatic life.

Underwater Photography

Wrecks make dramatic backgrounds for photos of divers and wildlife, and the wrecks themselves are usually photogenic — particularly fairly intact ones. Nondivers can often relate more easily to a picture of a recognizable wreck than to a natural reef simply because they see something with which they're familiar. In any case, underwater photographers (and videographers) find wrecks rewarding dive sites for the dramatic images they bring back.

Exercise 1

The Appeal of Wreck Diving

1. Divers may be interested in wreck diving because of (check all that apply):
   - ☐ a. curiosity
   - ☐ b. aquatic life
   - ☐ c. underwater photography
   - ☐ d. history

How did you do?
1. a., b., c., d.

Wreck Diving and the Law

Study Objectives

Underline/highlight the answers to these questions as you read:

1. What two primary considerations have led to the development of shipwreck laws?

2. Why shouldn't anyone except a trained archaeologist disturb artifacts on an historical wreck?

3. What are the two main arguments given against recreational divers removing objects and artifacts from nonhistorical wrecks?

4. What are the two main arguments given in favor of recreational divers removing, restoring and collecting objects and artifacts from nonhistorical wrecks?

5. Why does recovering an object require special training beyond the scope of the Wreck Diver course?

6. What is your responsibility with regard to laws that apply to the wrecks on which you dive?

The Origin of Shipwreck Laws

Laws regarding shipwrecks date back hundreds of years and were written for two primary reasons: to determine who had salvage rights, and (more recently) for antiquity protection.

Salvage laws determine who owns something that has been lost at sea. Most of these laws predate scuba diving, and state when a sunken ship (or other property) still belongs to the original owner, and when it's available to anyone willing to salvage it.

Most countries declare objects in the sea "up for grabs" when the owners abandon lost property, however, this doesn't necessarily make a wreck open to any diver who wants to take things off of it. Different areas have different salvage laws, and many owners and insurance companies still claim title for decades after a sinking. Even when salvage laws "clear" a wreck for partial or complete salvage, virtually all historical wrecks have legal protection.

Antiquity protection laws guard historical resources found underwater. Most of these were

Antiquity protection laws guard historical resources, including wrecks, so they can be studied by archaeologists.

3

written after the growth of scuba diving in the 1950s and 1960s, after divers ignorantly or uncaringly destroyed or damaged significant wreck sites before study by archaeologists. In the Mediterranean, for example, divers carried off amphorae (ancient earthen jars) from wrecks more than 2000 years old, often without even realizing they were diving on a wreck.

Today, divers have become much more aware of this problem, and legal artifact recovery for recreation takes place on nonhistorical wrecks. Still, most areas of the world now regulate what a diver may or may not do when visiting a particular wreck, or even whether someone may dive on a particular wreck at all.

As a rule of thumb, you can consider a wreck historical if it has known historical significance (the *Titanic*, for example), if it has been declared historical by law, or if it is more than approximately 100 years old (such as the remains of a Roman cargo ship).

Of course, use this only as a loose guideline. What constitutes an historical wreck varies from region to region as regulated by law. For example, many World War II Japanese wrecks now rest in Truk Lagoon, and while none of these are older than 100 years, and no individual ship has particular historical significance, the battle of Truk itself is very significant historically, and the law protects all the wrecks in the lagoon. In other areas, wrecks older than 100 years have been determined to have no historical value, and divers are free to visit them virtually unregulated.

The primary reason governments prohibit removing or even disturbing artifacts on historical wrecks is to preserve the site for archaeology. Archaeologists draw information not just from what they find in a wreck, but from where they find various objects in relation to one another. Simply picking up an old jar and moving it from one part of a wreck to another can destroy what the trained eye might have learned from it, even though the jar remains on the wreck.

To be clear, divers aren't the only source of wreck deterioration, nor even the most significant.

Storms, fishing nets and lines, current and the ravages of nature destroy wrecks over time. Notwithstanding, the archaeologist has enough trouble deciphering the puzzle eons and nature leave behind without having divers accidentally add to the problem.

Antiquity laws, then, basically spring from the philosophy that historical objects belong in muse-

Laws that protect archeological objects spring from the philosophy that such objects belong in museums to benefit the public.

ums and wrecks should benefit the public, rather than be harmed by people diving for fun or gathering objects for private collections. This doesn't slam the door on recreational divers, though, because

War Graves and Human Remains

While it's not common to come across human bones while wreck diving, it does happen, particularly when making penetration dives on war wrecks such as those found in the Pacific. If you ever discover human bones on a wreck:

1. Don't disturb them. In effect, you're visiting someone's final resting place, whether you intended to or not. Show the same respect you would visiting a cemetery. Some wrecks designated as war graves are closed to diving, but many are not, and probably will remain open to divers as long as divers treat the site and remains with respect.

2. If you think you're the first to discover remains on a particular wreck, report your find to the proper authorities. If it is an older historical wreck, the remains may have archaeological significance. If it is a more recent wreck, authorities may want to recover the bones for reburial elsewhere.

most wrecks — especially recent ones, don't have historical significance. However, be sure you know the laws and regulations before you disturb anything; if in doubt, leave everything on a wreck as you find it. Even well meaning actions can carry a penalty: a diver was once fined for removing a modern soda can (litter) from a protected wreck site.

Controversy surrounds collecting artifacts found on wrecks. Those who oppose artifact collection point out that a wreck is more interesting with artifacts in place. Those who advocate collection point out that the wreck and its artifacts eventually deteriorate if left underwater indefinitely.

The Controversy Over Removing Artifacts from Nonhistorical Wrecks

Where legal, some divers like to wreck dive to find and recover artifacts from nonhistorical wrecks. However, this activity isn't part of the PADI Wreck Diver course, and in many areas, you'll find local divers highly discourage it.

Two schools of thought surround collecting, recovering and restoring wreck artifacts as a hobby, and in many areas, legal decisions about what constitutes an historical wreck or a public resource affect this practice, too. Those who argue against artifact collecting argue that once removed from the water, artifacts deteriorate rapidly if not properly preserved. This may lead to total loss of the artifact. They also point out that wrecks stripped of their artifacts are much less interesting for divers, so artifact removal eventually reduces the number of interesting wrecks to dive on.

Those who believe that artifact removal is acceptable if done responsibly, argue that many underwater environments rapidly destroy wrecks and artifacts. Therefore, if a diver recovers something and properly preserves it, it will be saved from inevitable loss. If displayed, more people — especially nondivers — will see the artifact than if it stayed on the wreck. Those who argue that artifact removal is acceptable also point out that the desire to collect artifacts motivates private individuals to research and look for wrecks, thus increasing the number of wreck diving sites available. No one might find these wrecks otherwise because neither governments nor museums have sufficient funds to locate them.

Like many issues, the controversy over removing artifacts doesn't have any black or white answers. The appropriateness of removing something from a wreck depends on many issues, including the wrecks in question, how many divers visit the wrecks, local laws, whether the diver will properly preserve and restore what he recovers, and other issues.

Regardless, artifact recovery often requires special training in raising an object, and in restoring and preserving an object. Both of these lie outside the scope of this course. Those interested in this activity should approach it responsibly and within applicable laws. The PADI Search & Recovery course teaches proper lift bag rigging and use (it's also covered in the Advanced Open Water program elective Search & Recovery dive), which applies to recovering heavier artifacts. Programs in underwater archaeology teach individuals how to restore and preserve what they bring up.

Your Responsibility and Wreck Laws

Clearly, laws affect many of the wrecks you're likely to visit. On some, virtually no regulations apply, and on others regulation may be strict. Some wrecks may be entirely closed to divers, while others may be open but require a permit. In any case, your

Laws affecting wreck diving vary from region to region. It's your responsibility to know and follow local laws.

Wreck Diving World Hot Spots: Scapa Flow

One of the world's premier wreck sites lies in the remote Orkney Islands off the northern tip of Scotland. It was here in Scapa Flow that the German High Fleet — 74 warships — was interned at the end of World War I.

Photo by Alan Webb

Admiral Ludwig Von Reuter, who commanded the fleet, believed that Germany would reject the Treaty of Versailles and the war would resume. Rather than let the ships fall into British hands, he ordered all the ships to scuttle. On June 21, 1919, all 74 ships — battleships, battle cruisers, cruisers, destroyers and their support ships — went to the bottom of Scapa Flow without so much as a bullet being fired.

Later, during World War II, the German U-47 U-boat under the command of Gunther Prien snuck into Scapa Flow, torpedoed two vessels and escaped. Subsequently, the Royal Navy sank derelict vessels strategically in the flow to block another U-boat from sneaking in.

Although many of the World War I and World War II vessels have been salvaged, many remain. One, the *Royal Oak* (torpedoed by the U-47) went down with hundreds of sailors aboard and, as a war grave, is closed to diving. However, remaining World War I German ships and block ships remain open to divers. Some of the block ships rise above the surface, so you can make a "shore" dive from the ship deck to the submerged portions of the wreck.

Scapa Flow is colder water, making a visit there seasonal, with dry suits recommended. However, cooler water deteriorates wrecks much more slowly than tropical water. For this reason, many Scapa Flow World War I wrecks are in better condition than World War II wrecks in tropical water.

responsibility as a wreck diver includes finding out what laws apply before you go diving, and obeying those laws while you dive.

Exercise 2

Wreck Diving and the Law

1. The two primary considerations that have led to the development of shipwreck laws are:

    ☑ a. antiquity protection ☐ c. diver safety

    ☐ b. artificial reef preservation ☑ d. salvage rights

2. You shouldn't disturb an historically significant wreck because archaeologists learn a great deal from how objects lie in relation to each other.

    ☑ True ☐ False

3. The two main arguments against removing objects and artifacts from nonhistorical wrecks are (check two):

    ☐ a. it causes a substantial reduction of underwater habitat

    ☑ b. it may lead to the complete loss of the artifact

    ☐ c. it may be dangerous to the diver

    ☑ d. it leaves less for subsequent divers to see

4. The two main arguments given in favor of removing, restoring and collecting objects and artifacts from nonhistorical wrecks are (check two):

    ☑ a. the environment destroys artifacts over time anyway, so collection and proper treatment preserves them

    ☑ b. collecting artifacts creates the incentive to find wrecks, thus creating new dive sites

    ☐ c. collecting artifacts saves local government money because it doesn't have to hire archaeologists to do it.

    ☐ d. collecting artifacts makes wrecks safer by removing obstructions

5. Artifact recovery requires special training beyond the scope of this course, including (check all that apply):

    ☑ a. artifact preservation

    ☑ b. lift bag use

    ☑ c. artifact restoration

6. It's not necessary to check wreck diving laws if you don't intend to disturb or remove anything from a wreck.

    ☐ True ☑ False

How did you do?
1. a, d. 2. True. 3. b, d. 4. a, b. 5. a, b, c. 6. False. Divers may be entirely prohibited from diving on some wrecks.

Wreck Diving Hazards

Hazards Common to Most Wrecks

Like all dive environments, shipwrecks have potential hazards that you'll want to watch for and avoid. As long as you remain alert, keeping clear of these hazards shouldn't be a significant problem. While some wrecks have hazards unique to the wreck, there are five hazards common to many wrecks.

Sharp objects

Rusted metal, jagged steel plates, broken glass, splintering wood and rough or sharp coral all pose potential injury sources to an unwary diver. Even when diving a wreck sunk intentionally as an artificial reef, these hazards develop over time as the environment deteriorates the wreck's structure.

Your exposure suit helps you avoid most sources of potential cuts or abrasions. In addition,

Rusted metal may be abrasive and have sharp edges. Wear an exposure suit and gloves when wreck diving to minimize the chance of scrapes or cuts.

it's wise to wear protective gloves, even if you prefer not to wear them on natural reefs. The potential for cuts tends to be greater on wrecks, and there's more tendency to use your hands because you can often pull yourself along more readily than on a natural reef without damaging aquatic life. It's recommended that you keep your tetanus immunizations current in the event of an accidental cut.

Entanglement

Wrecks attract fish, which makes them popular sites for both commercial and sport fishing. When you go diving, expect wrecks to have monofilament fishing line or fishing nets on them, plus possibly ropes, cables and other lines used aboard them.

You can avoid possible entanglement by remaining alert. Look up as well as around so you don't accidentally swim under a net or thick concentrations of line. Stay well away from any significant accumulations of fishing net, and pay close attention to the taller parts of the wreck, which tend to catch the most line.

Carry a sharp knife with a smooth and serrated edge so you can cut your way free of entanglement too difficult to untangle by hand. Many experienced wreck divers wear two or more knives — a large, general purpose knife or tool, and a smaller, very sharp backup, emergencies-only knife. For additional security, wear the knives widely separated, such as one inside your calf and the other on your BCD, to help ensure you can reach at least one if entangled.

Entanglement may be a problem on some wrecks, especially if you inadvertently swim under concentrations of net or line.

Aquatic life

Since wrecks quickly become artificial reefs, you need to keep an eye out for the same creatures that defensively sting or bite on local natural reefs. Follow the same procedures you learned during your Open Water Diver course: watch where you put your hands, feet and knees; wear exposure protection; and don't touch unfamiliar animals.

Unstable structure

As a wreck ages, its walls, keel and hull weaken. Slowly, but surely, the wreck collapses into pieces. Although a wreck's collapse progresses slowly and steadily, the final fall of each piece happens quickly, usually when strong current, surge or high seas break away the weakened part. You can dive on a wreck, then return shortly after a storm and find

Do not touch, move or disturb munitions found underwater. Divers have lost their lives by accidentally triggering explosives.

superstructure completely torn from it. When hurricane Andrew hit south Florida in 1992, it actually moved entire wrecks and knocked upright wrecks on to their sides.

Although the final stress that breaks weak structure usually comes from a storm or current, it can also come from a careless diver. The hazard, of course, is that part of the wreck could fall on (especially if penetrating a wreck) or trap a diver. Falling wreckage can also pull fishing lines or nets over a diver.

Avoid this hazard by staying completely away from unstable structure. Look for walls or super-structure that move in the current or surge, give easily when touched, or simply look unstable. Give these areas a wide berth. You normally find such unstable structure only in isolated parts of a wreck, but you can come across wrecks that appear unstable throughout. It's usually best to avoid diving on such wrecks.

War wrecks may have munitions in them or lying around them, and these may be located in an unstable area, or may be unstable themselves depending on how they lie. Even after decades underwater, these munitions can still be explosive.

 Do not touch, move or disturb munitions found underwater. Divers have lost their lives by accidentally triggering explosives.

Surge pockets and suction

In surge conditions, water movement through a wreck can cause periodic suction through restricted openings such as hatches and holes. The wreck may draw and expel water in cycles as waves roll over, particularly if the wreck sticks partially above the surface.

Be cautious around wreck openings when you have surge present. Before swimming in front of one, watch suspended particles to see if they get pulled into the wreck, or stick your hand ahead carefully to feel for suction. If you encounter suction, it's usually best to stay clear of the area and explore other parts of the wreck.

Hazards of Wreck Penetration

In diving, overhead environments that block or restrict a vertical ascent to the surface pose significant hazard. Cavern diving/cave diving and ice diving necessarily involve entering an overhead environment, whereas in wreck diving, penetrating

Overhead environments can look deceptively safe and simple, yet without the proper equipment and training in specialized techniques, there's a significant risk of a fatal accident if you enter one.

the wreck is optional.

No diver should take entering a wreck (or any overhead environment) lightly; overhead environments can look deceptively safe and simple, yet without the proper equipment and training in the specialized techniques, divers can have accidents — all too often fatal ones.

It's worth noting what hazards await the diver inside a wreck, if only to emphasize the grave importance of never attempting a penetration dive without the proper training and equipment. You'll learn about the special equipment and techniques for limited wreck penetration later in this manual and in the PADI Wreck Diver course. However, understand that even with the proper equipment, training and procedures, entering a wreck raises potential risk and stress, which may reduce your fun and enjoyment.

Loss of direction

Perhaps the most immediate hazard in a wreck or other overhead environment is getting lost, and it's easier than you may imagine. A diver can lose his sense of direction merely by entering a wreck, aggravated further if the wreck lies on it's side or even leans off an even keel.

Inside the wreck, collapsed passages and debris may block logical paths, and open strange ones, so a diver can't rely on intuition. The wreck may look simple and logical on the outside, but inside may be a three dimensional maze with limited visibility. If a diver loses his way, he must find the way out before he runs out of air. Unfortunately, divers have lost their way in wrecks and not made it out.

No direct access to the surface

Even if a diver doesn't lose his direction, an overhead environment denies the safety of ascending immediately if he has a problem. In a low air or out of air situation, the diver doesn't have the options of making a controlled emergency swimming ascent or a buoyant ascent. If divers must share air, they must negotiate their way out of the wreck before ascending. The only way *up* is *out*.

Restricted passages

Inside a wreck, the careless diver can swim down a dead end passage, only to find he doesn't have enough room to turn around. Restrictions have more potential for hitting sharp or abrasive objects, impeding turns and obstructing buddy assistance.

Note: Even when making penetrations using appropriate equipment and techniques, avoid these type of passages completely.

Falling objects

In some wrecks, a diver can dislodge objects that fall on the diver or block his way. If a large object falls behind a diver, it can interfere with exiting. Divers making penetration dives must avoid any area that has the potential for falling objects.

Silt

Silt (particulate matter) tends to accumuate on most wrecks, especially inside. Stirring silt with fins,

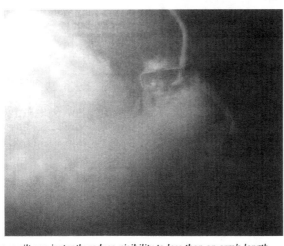

Stirring up silt can instantly reduce visibility to less than an arm's length.

hands or equipment can cause a dangerous "silt out" — a complete or nearly complete loss of visibility caused by clouding the water. Even exhaust bubbles can obscure visibility by dislodging silt on the wreck walls and ceilings. Silt outs can reduce unrestricted visibility to zero in moments, and frequently lead to disorientation and direction loss. This can leave the unprepared diver in the precarious situation of having to find his way out before he runs out of air.

As you'll learn, proper equipment and procedures, and staying within appropriate limits, make it possible to enter wrecks without significant risk. However, *never* **enter a wreck or other overhead environment without the proper training and equipment, and without following the proper procedures.**

Wreck Diving World Hot Spots: Bermuda

Lying on the trade route from Europe to North America and surrounded by many shallow, hard to spot reefs, over the years Bermuda has accumulated more than its share of wrecks. It's probably the only place in the world where you can find 350 wrecks spanning 400 years of sea faring in proximity. You can dive on modern, nearly intact ships that have been underwater less than 20 years, and on ancient broken up wrecks that have been underwater for centuries — sometimes on a single boat trip.

Bermuda lies in the "cool tropics" — 32 degrees North Latitude, but within the warming influence of the Gulf Stream. Compared with many wreck locations, Bermuda allows more relaxing dives with less insulation re-

quired, generally shallower depths, and seldom problems with strong current. You'll also find the Bermuda Maritime Museum with the Teddy Tucker Treasure Collection, which features treasure, shipwreck artifacts and dive equipment from

the 1950s and 1960s. Note: Only archaeologists authorized by the government may remove artifacts from Bermuda shipwrecks. Other divers may visit most wrecks, but may not disturb anything.

Exercise 3

Wreck Diving Hazards

1. Potential hazards common to many wrecks include (check all that apply):
   - ☑ a. sharp objects
   - ☑ b. entanglement
   - ☑ c. surge pockets
   - ☑ d. aquatic life
   - ☑ e. unstable structure
2. Hazards of wreck penetration include (check all that apply):
   - ☑ a. loss of direction
   - ☑ b. no direct access to the surface
   - ☑ c. silt
   - ☑ d. restricted passages
   - ☑ e. falling objects

How did you do?
1. a, b, c, d, e.   2. a, b, c, d, e.

Study Objectives

Underline/highlight the answers to these questions as you read:

1. What are four aspects of a wreck to evaluate when diving on it?

2. What are three ways to navigate on a wreck?

3. Why may a compass be inaccurate on a wreck?

4. What four dive planning and equipment considerations should be made for wreck dives deeper than 18 metres/60 feet?

5. What are the general techniques for wreck diving in a current?

6. What are two reasons why you should obtain a local orientation for an unfamiliar wreck?

Wreck Diving Techniques

Evaluating a Wreck

When you dive on a wreck for the first time, it's a good idea to look the wreck over and get to know it. On a large ship, it often takes several dives just to see the whole wreck, so becoming familiar with a wreck progresses each time you dive on it.

Although you become familiar with any dive site instinctively, you speed up familiarity with a wreck by consciously evaluating four aspects of its condition. Even after you become acquainted with it, you'll want to informally evaluate these each time you visit.

Possible hazards

Look for the hazards you just read about, and any hazards unique to the wreck. This allows you to plan subsequent dives to avoid them.

Points of interest

All wrecks have their highlights and areas that stand apart as points of interest. Look for unique features that give the wreck its personality. A ship's

Prominent, recognizable artifacts stand out as points of interest on a wreck, but don't overlook equally interesting, less conspicuous features.

wheel, telegraph, anchor or bell may be a prominent feature, but don't forget the natural aspects as well.

A wreck's condition affects the way you explore it, and may affect your safety.

A large moray eel that lives in the wreck, for instance, can be as interesting as the ship itself.

General condition

The wreck's condition affects the way you explore it, areas you may wish to avoid and your safety, especially if you're considering a penetration dive. Check whether the walls and structure appear strong and intact, or flimsy and unstable. Look for any structure or objects that might be ready to fall. Consider the wreck's condition against its age, the environment and its material. An old wooden wreck may be quite sound even after a hundred years in cold fresh water, yet a metal wreck in turbulent tropical water may be ready to collapse in a decade.

Entryways

If you're considering a subsequent penetration dive, look for suitable ways to enter the wreck. Appropriate entries are large, unobstructed openings that admit much light. Rule out any entry that requires a tight squeeze, removing equipment or tying back a door or hatch. You'll want an opening large enough to swim through comfortably, and free of sharp objects, blockage or other hazards.

Navigating on wrecks

In most circumstances, navigating on a wreck is easier than navigating on a natural reef. You usually don't go as far when diving on a wreck, and intact wreck structure makes natural navigation easier.

When diving on a large, broken up wreck, however, navigation may not be so straightforward. You'll find wreck navigation influenced by how familiar you are with the wreck, your dive objective and how much of the wreck you plan to explore. Depending on its condition and what you find when you evaluate it, there are three basic ways to navigate on a wreck. In some cases, you may find it advantageous to use different techniques on the same wreck as you move from one area to another. Sometimes it helps to use these techniques simultaneously.

Follow the wreck's layout

On a fairly intact wreck, it's usually easiest to follow the ship's natural lines, such as by swimming along the hull or a rail. This works well in limited visibility as well as in clear water, and is one of the easiest ways to find your way on a wreck.

On smaller wrecks, such as a tugboat, you can navigate and see the entire wreck by following the hull around the perimeter. On larger ships, you can swim along one side until you reach your turn point (no decompression time or air supply), then swim

An intact wreck makes navigation easy. Simply follow the natural layout of the ship.

across the wreck and follow the other side back to your start point.

Feature reference

When diving a broken up and scattered wreck, you probably won't find the same natural lines to follow as on an intact wreck. Instead, you navigate by noting prominent features and their relative positions to track where you are and find your way back.

When diving in relatively clear, currentless water on a wreck with relatively few conspicuous features, navigating by memory usually suffices. In reduced visibility, when the wreckage lies scattered over a wide area, or on a wreck with many features that you could confuse, it's worth taking the time to sketch/note your path to simplify returning to your start point. As you swim through the various features, look back periodically so you can see how they'll look when navigating back.

Although you normally use feature reference for navigating broken up wrecks, you may find it useful on large intact wrecks of major ships. Major ships may have multiple features that look similar, particularly along adjacent decks. Feature reference helps keep you from confusing, for example, a row of pipes you were following with a similar row a deck up.

When navigating a large, broken up wreck, look for conspicuous features that can help you find your way.

Base line

Base line navigation uses a straight line you draw through a wreck; you'll find it especially useful on a very scattered and broken up wreck with few prominent features. The base line forms a known heading back to the anchor/mooring line or exit that you track constantly during the dive. You swim along the line, leaving it for short distances to explore, then returning to it as you continue through the wreck.

For a wreck in clear, currentless water, you may use an informal general direction through the wreckage as a base line. In more restricted visibility, you may want to use a more precise compass heading, and in poor visibility, or with a current, you may want to lay out a rope for you and your fellow divers to follow. The more challenging the conditions, the more precise you'll want your base line. (Note: Keep in mind that iron and steel objects may affect compass readings by attracting the magnetic needle away from north. Don't expect your compass to read as accurately as usual.)

Considerations for Deeper Wrecks

As you probably recall from the PADI Advanced Open Water program, dives deeper than 18 metres/60 feet call for deep diving procedures and equipment. You'll find many wrecks shallower than 18 metres/60 feet, but the majority of larger wrecks lie deeper, primarily because large ships cruise oceans and major lakes well away from shore to avoid striking reefs. When an accident happens, therefore, large ships often sink in deep water.

It's recommended that you consider the following points when planning wreck dives deeper than 18 metres/60 feet:

1. Be trained as a PADI Deep Diver

The PADI Deep Diver course extends the training and experience you've had in the Advanced Open Water core deep dive, providing you with more hands-on experience with deep diving techniques and equipment. In fact, divers interested in wreck diving often make up the majority of students in a PADI Deep Diver program. See your PADI Dive Center, Resort or Instructor about this course.

2. Hang a tank at 5 metres/15 feet

This assures ample air for a safety stop or an emergency decompression stop if you encounter a delay returning to your ascent line, or if you use air more rapidly than you planned. Be sure you can relocate your ascent line (which may be an anchor/mooring line), and that you have any other deep diving equipment appropriate for the local environment.

3. Take the effect of narcosis into account

As you approach 30 metres/100 feet, you can expect nitrogen narcosis to affect you, even if you don't particularly notice it. Plan the dive accordingly by keeping your objectives simple, avoiding task loading and giving yourself ample time.

Don't change your dive plan during a deep dive in a way that makes the dive less conservative. For example, if you planned a maximum 20 minutes dive time, it's acceptable to surface at 15 minutes, but don't change your mind and stay 25 minutes. Following this guideline reduces the possibility of narcosis affecting your judgment in an unsafe way.

In restricted visibility or a current, you may want to lay out a rope to use as a base line for navigation.

A tank at 5 metres/15 feet assures ample air for a safety stop or emergency decompression stop.

4. Plan for reduced bottom time

Available time diminishes rapidly below 18 metres/ 60 feet thanks to short no decompression limits and rapid air consumption. Plan your dive to stay closer to your ascent point than you would on a comparable shallow wreck.

On a tall, intact wreck, it's sometimes possible to moor or anchor into the wreck's top area. Using a dive computer or The Wheel, you can gain more bottom time by planning a multilevel dive that begins by descending to the deepest point you plan to explore on the wreck and gradually working your way back toward the surface in levels. However, avoid "sawtooth" dive profiles that involve ascending to a significantly shallower portion on the wreck, then having to drop back down to locate and ascend the anchor/mooring line.

Wreck Diving in Currents

Just as you commonly come across wrecks in deeper depths, you also commonly find them in areas with current. Current diving calls for special procedures, which vary from region to region and boat to boat. With only a few exceptions, such as drift diving, most dive boats use roughly similar techniques for wreck diving in currents.

The dive begins by anchoring the boat in the wreck, or attaching to a permanent mooring over the wreck. The crew then secures various lines to make it easier to reach the wreck and avoid getting swept down current. Off the stern they run a long *trail line* (also called "drift line" or "current line") with a float at the end. In all but the weakest currents, the dive boat also runs a *swim line* from the stern, trail line or entry area to the anchor/mooring line.

You enter the water and use the swim line to pull yourself against the current to the anchor/ mooring line. If you need to wait for your buddy, you either wait on the trail line, or you move up the swim line and let him follow you. In strong currents, you may hold the swim line while you enter.

When you and your buddy reach the anchor/ mooring line, you descend hand over hand to the wreck. (Note: Permanent mooring lines tend to

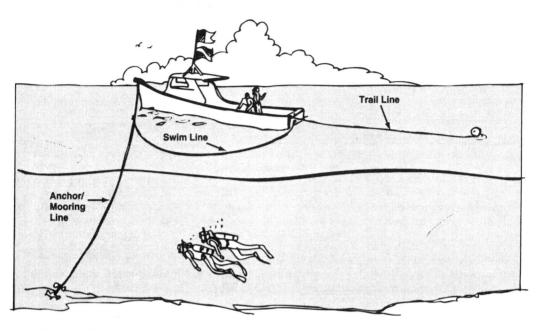

Current diving procedures vary, but basically call for pulling yourself along the swim line *to the* anchor/mooring line, *which you follow down to the wreck. At the end of the dive, ascend along the* anchor/mooring line, *then follow the* swim line *to the boat ladder or swim step. Wait for your turn to board on the* trail line.

become encrusted with aquatic growth, so watch where you put your hands and wear gloves for protection.) The current will usually be slower near the bottom, and most wrecks shelter you from the current on the lee side. You usually explore along the lee side, and if necessary, pull yourself along the wreck, being cautious where you put your hands.

At the end of the dive, return to the anchor/ mooring line and ascend along it. Make your safety stop at 5 metres/15 feet, then continue back up to the swim line. Follow the swim line back to the stern, exit point or trail line — to whichever it's secured. You want to maintain contact with the lines at all times during your descent and ascent. However, the trail line extends the boat in case a diver surfaces alongside or gets swept off a line and has to swim for the boat in the current. It also provides you a place to wait for your turn to exit. As an added precaution, it's a good idea to carry an inflatable signal tube in case you end up down current so you can signal the boat to pick you up.

Why Hand Pulling Works

You only have to pull yourself along a rope in current once to realize that it's *much* more effective than swimming, but it may not be obvious *why.* After all, your legs have more strength than your arms — shouldn't fin kicks be more effective?

Try this with a buddy while floating at the surface in calm water: With neither of you using your feet, gently push away from your buddy with your arms, and note how far you drift from where you started. Now do the same thing against a fixed object, like a pool side

or dock. You'll drift (give or take, depending on your buddy's size relative to yours) about twice as far.

When pushing against your buddy, he moves away from the start point about as much as you do. In other words, about half your directed energy goes into moving you, and the other half into moving him. This is like using fins — about half the energy of each kick goes into moving you, and the other half goes into moving the water you kick against.

When pushing against the pool side, all your directed energy goes into

moving you because the pool side can't move. This is like pulling yourself along a rope or over a wreck — virtually all of your pull goes into moving you because you're directing your energy against a fixed object.

In addition, you can't rest in a current while swimming. If you stop swimming, you get swept down current and have to expend energy to get back to where you stopped. When pulling yourself, you just stop and hang on. Your pulling muscles rest and you don't lose ground.

Local Orientations to Unfamiliar Wrecks

Wreck diving varies from region to region and from wreck to wreck. As a PADI Wreck Diver, you'll be familiar with the basic techniques for exploring wrecks in recreational diving environments, but get a local orientation to unfamiliar wrecks whenever possible.

One reason a local orientation helps is that the optimum techniques may differ locally from the ones you're used to. A local orientation shows you the particular procedures that work well in the area, or on a specific wreck.

The second reason for getting a local orientation is to enhance your dive. A local orientation lets you know about a wreck's unique points of interest and its hazards in advance. This makes it easier to plan your dive. If you'll only have a chance to make one or two dives on the wreck, it steers you to the best spots on it.

WRECK DIVING TECHNIQUES

Wreck Diving World Hot Spots: North American Great Lakes

The Great Lakes on the border between the U.S. and Canada hold some of the best preserved major shipwrecks in the world. Although they're freshwater bodies, the Great Lakes are really inland seas,

the Great Lakes since the 1500s, with commercial traffic common by the end of the 18th century. During the 1800s wooden frigates gave way to iron steamships, which evolved into today's steel freighters.

subject to violent storms that have sunk major ships more than 220 metres/700 feet long. The combined shoreline of Lakes Huron, Ontario, Erie, Michigan and Superior is greater than the entire U.S. Atlantic coastline.

Ships have been sailing

Estimates suggest that somewhere between 3000 and 10,000 wrecks lie in the Great Lakes. Those that divers have found tend to be very well preserved by the cold, fresh water. Even wooden ships remain remarkably intact after more

than 100 years underwater. Divers frequently find artifacts in remarkable condition (though most areas prohibit removing these). As wreck diving has grown popular in the Great Lakes, underwater parks and preserves have been established in both the U.S. and Canada to protect these wrecks. Some of the most popular include Alger Underwater Preserve, the Apostle Islands National Lakeshore, Devil's Door, Fathom Five National Park (a.k.a. "Tobermory"), Isle Royal National Park, and Manitou Passage Underwater Preserve.

The Great Lakes remain cool year round, calling for full wet suits or dry suits. Visibility changes depending on weather, and you can encounter moderate currents as well. Most divers visit wrecks by boat, but you can reach quite a few wrecks from shore. Dive depths range from snorkel depths to beyond the limits of recreational diving.

Exercise 4

Wreck Diving Techniques

1. Four aspects of a wreck to evaluate include (check all that apply):
    - ☑ a. points of interest
    - ☐ b. number of divers on the wreck
    - ☑ c. possible hazards
    - ☑ d. general condition
    - ☑ e. entry ways
    - ☐ f. recoverable artifacts

2. Which is not a common method for navigating on a wreck?
    - ☐ a. feature reference
    - ☐ b. base line
    - ☐ c. following the wreck's layout
    - ☑ d. dead reckoning

3. A compass may be inaccurate on a wreck because
    - ☑ a. steel and iron may cause the needle to deviate.
    - ☐ b. currents common around wrecks make it hard to keep a heading.

4. Wreck dives deeper than 18 metres/60 feet call for which of the following considerations (check all that apply):
    - ☑ a. accounting for nitrogen narcosis
    - ☑ b. certification as a PADI Deep Diver
    - ☑ c. planning for reduced bottom time
    - ☑ d. leaving emergency breathing equipment at 5 metres/15 feet

5. When wreck diving in a current, you'll generally drop straight to the bottom and avoid all contact with the boat's anchor/mooring line.
    - ☐ True
    - ☑ False

6. When diving on an unfamiliar wreck, there's not much benefit of a local orientation if you're a certified PADI Wreck Diver.
    - ☐ True
    - ☑ False

How did you do?
1. a, c, d, e.   2. d.   3. a.   4. a, b, c, d.   5. False. You generally descend and ascend along the anchor/mooring line to keep from being carried down current.   6. False. A local orientation to an unfamiliar wreck acquaints you with local techniques, points of interest and hazards.

Study Objectives

Underline/highlight the answers to these questions as you read:

1. What are three reasons for researching the history and condition of a wreck?

2. What two sources provide quick, basic information about diving a popular wreck?

3. What possible sources can you check when researching more in-depth, detailed wreck information?

Researching Underwater Wrecks

For many divers, wreck diving encompasses much more than visiting a ship underwater. It includes visiting the ship's past through research. To these individuals, exploring the local library, archive or museum is almost as exciting as exploring the wreck itself.

Whether conducting wreck research appeals to you depends, at least partly, on what draws you to wrecks in the first place. If wrecks interest you for their roles as artificial reefs, why a ship sank probably means less than if you're interested in wrecks from an historical perspective. In that case, uncovering the wreck's history may be something you consider a normal part of diving a wreck.

Either way, researching a wreck's history — at least minimally — benefits you in three basic ways when you dive the wreck. First, research uncovers the wreck's history and significance, and may explain the wreck's location and condition. If you're interested in nature, it's useful to know when the ship sank so you know how long aquatic life has been developing on it.

Second, research reveals or confirms a wreck's

Some divers find researching wrecks almost as exciting as actually diving wrecks.

identity, especially when dealing with a newly discovered wreck. Knowing what the wreck is plays an important role in determining whether the wreck has historical/archaeological significance, and whether it may have some unusual hazard to avoid, such as munitions.

Third, research helps you uncover unique points of interest, the suitability of the wreck as a dive site, and potential hazards. As you just learned, a local orientation usually covers these points, but research may uncover new facts, or help provide this information when you can't get a local orientation.

You can get wreck information from basic, readily available sources, and from more involved references that take more time and effort to locate. The basic sources apply to most popular wrecks, and generally provide what you need to know for diving purposes, such as the wreck's general history, condition and points of interest. Quick, basic wreck information sources include:

- Dive stores and dive boats. You can usually get a few facts about popular wrecks in their area, plus general wreck conditions, pointers and things to watch for.

- Diving magazines/guidebooks. Look for articles about popular wrecks, which usually include more detail and background information than you're likely to get from a dive store or boat. The drawback to this source is that you may have trouble finding an article on the particular wreck that interests you. They also become dated as the wreck deteriorates.

For more detail than you're likely to get from a local dive store or boat, and when you can't find a wreck's published history (such as with a newly discovered wreck), you may want to conduct some more involved research. You may also find it interesting to research a well known wreck, because sometimes the "facts" that divers pass on to each other are inaccurate. Sources of more in-depth wreck information can include:

- Libraries. Look up newspaper articles (they may be on microfilm) from the date of the wreck's sinking. As you scan through the papers, keep an eye out for references to other wrecks — you might uncover facts about an undiscovered wreck that no one has looked for.

- Museums. Write or visit maritime museums for specific information. These specialized museums maintain incredible volumes of files, photos and other information. Often, you can access more than you want to know just by identifying the ship. When possible, identify the ship by name, approximate age, sinking date (or approximate date, if known) and registry. The more information you provide, the more easily the museum can locate records if it has any.

- Archives. Write or visit the archives maintained by insurance companies, lighthouses, harbors and national history libraries/museums. Ask for specific information; you'll usually get a list of what they have available, from which you request items that interest you.

- Historical/archaeological groups. Local groups often know the history of regional events and wrecks in surprising detail.

- Maritime societies. These groups usually maintain records of members and their ships.

- Maritime insurance companies. Lloyds of London and other companies that insure ships keep records on every ship, past or present, floating or sunk, that they insure. When a ship sinks, filing the claim usually involves detailed reports of who, what, where, why and when.

First hand research usually turns up more accurate or more detailed information about a wreck than you'll get through casual conversations with other divers.

Don't hesitate to request information from sources like these — that's what they're there for. If people like you didn't ask, there wouldn't be any reason to have museums, libraries and archives. However, don't expect everything for free; most institutions like these operate on tight budgets, and while they don't try to make a profit, they often require you to cover the cost of photocopying, duplicating microfilm, etc.

Wreck Diving World Hot Spots: The Graveyard of the Atlantic

Off the United States' east coast lies the Graveyard of the Atlantic. Centered off North Carolina and reaching north of the Canadian border and south into Florida, this expanse harbors the remains of thousands of ships. Sunk by storms, torpedoes in both World Wars, collisions and other accidents, these ships have become very popular with wreck divers.

One reason is that the continental shelf extends far off the coast, so that wrecks more than 20 kilometres/10 miles offshore lie shallow enough for recreational diving. In addition, the Gulf Stream sweeps up the coast, so that many of the wrecks (especially more southern ones) are in warm tropical water much of the year. Currents are common and temperatures vary, however.

You can dive a wreck one day with minimal exposure protection and no current, and the next find yourself on the same wreck in a dry suit, hanging onto the anchor line against a moderate flow.

Most of the popular wrecks are from World War II (including a few U-boats), but not exclusively. Some, such as the *San Diego* and *Proteus* date back to the World War I era, while others, such as the *Tarpon*, sank much more recently.

Exercise 5

Researching Underwater Wrecks

1. Three reasons for researching the history and condition of a wreck are (check all that apply):
   - ☑ a. to determine the wreck's historical significance
   - ☑ b. to confirm the wreck's identity
   - ☐ c. to confirm the dive boat brought you to the right wreck
   - ☑ d. to determine points of interest and potential hazards before the dive

2. Two sources for quick, basic information about a popular wreck are:
   - ☐ a. archives
   - ☑ b. dive stores/boats
   - ☑ c. dive magazines
   - ☐ d. maritime museums
   - ☐ e. insurance companies

3. Sources for more in-depth, detailed wreck information include (check all that apply):
   - ☑ a. archives
   - ☐ b. dive stores/boats
   - ☐ c. dive magazines
   - ☑ d. maritime museums
   - ☑ e. insurance companies

How did you do?
1. a, b, d.   2. b, c.   3. a, d, e.

Study Objectives

Underline/highlight the answers to these questions as you read:

1. What are two benefits of mapping a wreck?

2. What four tools can you use when mapping a wreck, and what is each used for?

Mapping Shipwrecks

Although you probably won't map every wreck you dive on, from time to time you'll find it useful. Some divers like to map wrecks purely because they find mapping enjoyable, but there are two practical reasons for mapping wrecks.

The first is to simplify future dives. As you've already learned, two of the primary wreck characteristics you watch for are points of interest and potential hazards. By creating a wreck map, you can note these, updating and expanding the map (for a large wreck) from one dive to the next. Some divers keep copies of their maps at each stage, so they can show how the wreck has changed over time.

The second reason to map a wreck is for planning penetration dives. You use a wreck map to plan possible entries into the wreck, and, if you carry it with you (laminated in plastic or sketched onto a slate), it can help guide you through the wreck during the penetration.

Wreck Diving World Hot Spots: Where You Are

Besides the well known wreck diving hot spots previously described, you'll find numerous other areas with concentrations of wrecks: Australia's Victorian coast boasts more than 800 wrecks, and the Mediterrean holds thousands that span the centuries. Off the Atlantic coast of south Florida in the U.S., the dive community has created a wreck diving haven with its artifical reef program.

So, while you may dream of places like Truk Lagoon or Scapa Flow, don't overlook the opportunities right under your nose. The very fact that they're visited less by divers sometimes makes these dives more exciting than more famous, popular areas!

Basic Wreck Mapping Techniques

Over the years, divers have come up with perhaps dozens of methods for mapping wrecks. These range from archaeological methods, which require placing a grid over the wreck and mapping it with precision and detail square by square, to a rough sketch from memory. For most purposes, something in between suffices.

You'll find four tools useful for mapping.

- A large slate. Draw your map on as a large a slate as possible. Your map will be more accurate if you give yourself room to draw. If necessary for carrying, you can transfer your finished map to something smaller, or reduce it with a copy machine.

- Compass. Use this to determine the relative angle between different wreck features. Again,

Use a tape measure to find precise distances for your map; for coarse maps, arm spans and kick cycles will suffice.

A compass, Nav-Finder, and marked line or measuring tape come in handy for mapping wrecks.

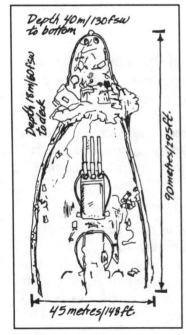

Note depths and distances on your finished map.

beware of compass deviation caused by steel or iron.

- Marked rope or measuring tape. Use a tape or marked line to give you precise distances between objects and features. You can also measure with kick cycles and arm spans. Tape/line gives you greater accuracy; kick cycles/ arm spans save you time.

- Navigational aids. The Nav-Finder, grids with finds and other aids help you sketch map features with greater accuracy, and save you time. You may also find them useful for general navigation on the wreck.

Draw your map using your compass to measure relative angles and measuring distance from one part to the next. As you sketch, try to draw everything to scale, but unless you take a ruler, that may be difficult. For that reason, note the measured length of each distance you draw, and note the relative angles from your compass. Later you can make a second draft with a ruler and protractor for better scale and angle precision.

For additional utility (especially if you share your map with other divers), you may want to include information in addition to the wreck's layout. Note depth at various points, especially at the bottom, on different deck levels and for prominent features. You may also want to include the Loran/GPS coordinates, or a miniature map inset with shore bearings for locating the wreck.

How to Mark a Wreck

When you wreck dive from a charter boat, finding the wreck is easy – you just enjoy the ride until the captain or divemaster announces your arrival. The crew *marks* (pinpoints) the wreck for you.

When diving from a private boat, you'll have to mark the wreck yourself. Marking a wreck is as much an art as a science — it sounds easy, but it takes practice, especially when dealing with wind or current. Minimally, you'll need a bottom finder that shows relief, and ideally, you will also have a Loran or GPS unit. A couple of marker buoys with sufficient line for the depth greatly simplify the job, too. If you have current, use an extra heavy anchor on the buoys so they deploy fast and don't drift far.

Begin by motoring to the wreck's coordinates (Loran, GPS or lined up shore bearings). As you approach the coordinates, slow down and watch the bottom finder, looking for a sharp spike or rise that indicates the wreck. (The taller the wreck and the flatter the bottom, the easier this will be.) If you're lucky or if you've gotten re-ally tight bearings (like GPS), you'll motor right up to the wreck; toss in a marker buoy when you do. Stay close to the buoy and tie it off as soon as it hits bottom so you don't get much slack.

If you miss the wreck, toss in and tie off a marker at the coordinates where it was supposed to be. Use this as a reference and begin searching away from it. In conditions with little current or wind, an expanding square pattern with the buoy at the center works well. With current or wind, initially try a U-pattern into the current or wind. Keep searching (and this can take a while) until you spot the wreck on your bottom finder. Toss in and tie off a second buoy.

Motor down current/downwind of the buoy marking the wreck, and have someone stand by the anchor. Motor directly toward and past the buoy (don't foul it in the props) until you spot the wreck on the bottom finder. Don't be surprised if you pass the buoy before you find it. Motor all the way across the wreck until you think you've cleared it, then hold the boat in place while someone lowers (not drops) the anchor quickly to the bottom. Put the engine in neutral and the current/wind should drift you back over the wreck and set the anchor. Try a touch of reverse engine to make sure it's holding.

Normally this procedure puts the anchor on the up current/up-wind side of the wreck, but not in it. To be *sure* you don't put the anchor in the wreck – important for old, historical or protected wrecks, motor until you first see the wreck on the bottom finder then, while someone begins lowering the anchor, ease off the power just enough so you drift back off of it, then increase power to stay in place. This puts the anchor down-wind/down current from the wreck.

Fair warning: This sounds easier than it is, especially when you're trying to mark a broken up wreck on an irregular bottom. Be patient, and if possible, practice with someone experienced at marking wrecks. Don't forget to pick up your buoys when you leave. Good luck.

Exercise 6

Mapping Shipwrecks

1. Two benefits of mapping shipwrecks include (check all that apply):
   - [ ] a. to note the current direction over the wreck
   - [x] b. to note points of interest and potential hazards
   - [x] c. to assist in planning penetration dives

2. Four tools that you can use in mapping a wreck are (check all that apply):
   - [x] a. large slate
   - [x] b. marked rope or tape measure
   - [x] c. navigational aids
   - [ ] d. nontoxic dye
   - [x] e. compass
   - [ ] f. anchor chain

How did you do?   *1. b, c.   2. a, b, c, e.*

Study Objectives

Underline/highlight the answers to these questions as you read:

1. What four pieces of equipment should be used for a penetration dive, and what is each piece used for?

2. What are the three penetration limits to observe when inside a wreck?

3. What are the proper techniques for:
   • Entering a wreck?
   • Moving through a wreck?
   • Using a penetration line in a wreck?

4. What are the proper responses and actions for:
   • Loss of visibility due to silting?
   • A lost or cut penetration line?
   • Light failure?
   • Air supply loss?

Fun and safe wreck penetration requires having the proper training and equipment, and staying within penetration limits.

Wreck Penetration

As you've already learned, entering a shipwreck (or any other overhead environment) presents many hazards you don't meet in open water. Because of this, many divers prefer to stay outside the wreck, avoiding the hazards and special equipment, training and procedures overhead environments require.

However, wreck penetration may interest you for the added challenge. If so, keep in mind that wreck penetration is a "do it right or don't do it all" activity. **Entering an overhead environment without the proper equipment and without following proper procedures may expose you to significant risk. It has taken hundreds of lives.** Never forget that many overhead environments look safe and unthreatening, yet pose grave danger to an unwary diver.

As a PADI Wreck Diver, you'll practice the techniques for safe, limited wreck penetration. Your training will be appropriate for penetrating a stable, secure wreck, within the light zone, in excellent environmental conditions, and applying all the needed equipment and procedures. Penetrating wrecks beyond the limits you learn in this program requires specialized technical or commercial diver training, and is beyond the scope of this course. Don't exceed your training/experience limits.

Wreck Penetration Equipment

Offsetting the hazards unique to penetration requires additional equipment beyond what you need to dive safely in open water. None of the following equipment is particularly complex, and you may already have most of it. However, without the necessary equipment, you shouldn't attempt a penetration dive.

Dive lights

Although you will remain within the light zone (area

from which you can still see the natural light at the entrance), ambient light dims as you move away from the entry. Therefore, you'll need *at least* two dive lights — a primary light and a backup. Many wreck divers carry no fewer than three dive lights during penetration dives.

You carry a backup light in case your primary

When penetrating a wreck, you'll want a larger primary light, and one or two smaller back up lights in case you have a problem with your primary.

light fails, of course. Compared with your other dive equipment, lights are some of the least reliable. This isn't the fault of the manufacturers (who have considerably improved the reliability and quality of dive lights in the past twenty years), but the nature of lights: bulbs burn out, batteries wear out, and the lights themselves flood occasionally, even with proper care.

By properly maintaining your lights and their O-rings, and making sure you have fresh (or freshly recharged) batteries before you dive, you minimize the possibility a light will fail, but a statistical look shows how important it is to carry a backup: Suppose your light is 95 percent reliable. That sounds pretty reliable, but you have *a 72 percent chance of light failure within 25 dives.* Even if your light were 99 percent reliable, you would still have about a 22 percent chance — about one in five — that it would fail within 25 dives. However, if you have two lights that are 95 percent reliable, the chances are about six percent, or one in 16, that both will fail on the same dive in 25 dives. If you have three such lights, the chances drop to one in 320, and with four, chances are only 1 in about 6450 that you'll have all four fail on the same dive within 25 dives. It's not hard to see why experienced wreck divers carry three or four lights, rather than the minimum two.

Carry your backup dive lights so that they're out of the way, yet accessible with one hand. This makes it possible to switch lights while using the other hand for maintaining buddy contact or penetration line contact. Most wreck divers find it simplest to attach a clip to the dive light, and then clip the light to a ring on the BCD.

Penetration line and reel

The penetration line provides a visual/tactile reference for finding your way out of the wreck, even if you're confused or unable to see due to silt. Statistics show that the most common cause of fatalities in overhead environments is a failure to run a continuous line to open water; never make a penetration dive without this line and a proper reel for handling it.

Line —— Wrecks frequently have sharp or abrasive surfaces than can sever your line, so use a strong, durable line made from a nonbiodegradable material. By far, nylon is the most popular choice because it doesn't float, it's durable and it handles well.

Many instructors and novice wreck divers use "beginner's line," which is normally twisted or braided .6 centimetre/.25 inch or larger nylon line. Rope this size stands up to abuse, such as a diver pulling himself through the wreck (not a proper procedure), and it doesn't tangle easily. However, large line requires a large, bulky and awkward reel. This is a good choice for inexperienced wreck divers making very limited penetrations.

Standard line is relatively thin braided nylon line (generally #36 line). You can carry more of this line on a smaller reel than beginner's line, but it tangles more easily and requires more care in use. Although standard line stands up to a surprising amount of abuse, it's not as strong as beginner's line, so you must place it properly and make sure no one uses it to pull himself along.

Divers new to wreck penetration sometimes prefer a large diameter line that's easy to handle. Divers with more penetration experience prefer a finer line that fits on a more compact reel.

Reels — For beginner's line, you'll usually use a large plastic reel or line caddie. Because of their size, you generally have to hand carry them throughout the dive, and they take two hands to use, even when paying out line. For the smaller braided line, you'll probably use a standard reel, which generally requires two hands only when reeling line in. Standard reels clip easily to your BCD, and they lock so they don't unreel unexpectedly.

Whether you're using a standard line and reel or beginner's, inspect your penetration line before each use. Discard any line that looks frayed, abraded or damaged in any way.

Slate

Earlier you learned that it's a good idea to carry a wreck map when making a penetration dive. You can sketch the map on your slate for reference during the penetration. As you go through the dive, you can make an interior map with notes to aid planning future penetration dives.

Slates also come in handy for communication, especially if you find yourself in an awkward spot that makes it difficult to face your buddy for signalling. You want to avoid restricted areas like these, but if you find yourself in one by accident, you can write a message to pass to your buddy.

Tips on Clips

The extra equipment you carry on a penetration dive makes accessory clips for attaching it to your BCD especially useful. While clips are straightforward items, here are some hints to get maximum utility from them.

- **Brass or plastic.** You can get accessories clips in brass, plastic and chrome plated. Field experience shows that some types of chrome plated don't hold up as well as brass or plastic. Many divers prefer brass, but plastic clips work well for lightweight items, and they don't add much to your load.
- **Sliding gate clips.** Most divers use either sliding gate clips or swinging gate quick clips. You have to open sliding gate clips (a.k.a. "dog clips") to attach them, whereas swinging gate clips snap right onto lines or BCD D rings. That's exactly why most wreck divers prefer sliding gate clips — swinging gate clips have a reputation for snapping onto penetration lines, cable and other things snagging a diver. In some areas, divers call quick clips "suicide" clips, in reference to the possible hazard they create.
- **Clip on the accessory.** You will find it handiest to put clips on your accessories, rather than on your BCD. With a clip on each light, reel, etc., you know there is a clip for each, plus you can easily move them to various D rings, loops and other places on your BCD.

Sliding gate clips are the preferred choice for wreck penetrations because they're less likely to clip themselves onto something accidentally.

Pony bottle

Although pony bottles aren't considered mandatory for all penetration dives, in some areas and wrecks, you may find that local divers consider them standard equipment. In any case, they're highly recommended in addition to your standard alternate air source second stage or alternate inflator regulator.

Pony bottles, which are miniature scuba tanks with their own regulators, equip you with a completely independent air source. This adds a safety margin for the overhead environment because, in the event of an air supply problem, it's easier to exit a wreck using your own pony bottle than sharing air with your buddy. The deeper the wreck, the more important this extra margin may be.

Pony bottles are highly recommended additions to your standard alternate air source second stage or alternate inflator regulator when making penetrations because they provide a completely independent air source.

Wreck Penetration Limits

Besides the equipment you need, the overhead environment imposes three limits that you should

Optional Penetration Equipment Configurations

Depending on the environment and the particular wreck, you may find the following ideas useful when setting up your equipment for penetration dives.

- **Two weight belt buckles.** In cool water environments, you may need a full wet suit or dry suit. This calls for a lot of weight to attain neutral buoyancy. Although you should consider a quick release primary safety equipment for open water diving, in an overhead environment, you wouldn't want to accidentally lose a heavy weight belt because extreme buoyancy could make it difficult to exit the wreck. As a precaution, some divers put two buckles on their belt, and clamp the extra one shut

when they enter the wreck. Upon leaving the wreck, they release the extra, restoring the ability to ditch their weights quickly with one hand.
- **Head lights.** Some divers like to mount lights on their heads. This frees their hands and the light always points where they're looking. Some lights have mounting straps especially for this purpose, plus many lights mount easily on helmets, which provide some protection. When using a head mounted light, remember that it's easier to accidentally shine the light in your buddy's eyes.
- **Snorkel quick release clip.** It's important to have your snorkel in case you need to make a long surface swim, even one that's

not part of your dive plan. Although you can carry a snorkel many places, the most accessible spot is on your mask strap. However, some divers prefer to get rid of their snorkels for penetration dives to avoid tangling or bumping into overhead obstacles. The optimum solution is to use the quick connect/disconnect snorkel clips available from several manufacturers. Before entering the wreck, unclip the snorkel and leave it secured to your penetration line tie point. When you return, clip it back on and you're ready to handle a surface swim. Snorkels at your tie point also alert other divers that your line is a penetration line, not a hazard they should cut out of the way.

observe when penetrating a wreck, in addition to the no decompression limits and depth limits you observe when diving in open water.

1. Edge of light zone.
Stay within sight of the natural light where you entered the wreck. This means that the available natural light may limit your penetration. If you're diving in relatively murky, low visibility conditions, less light enters the wreck and you may not be able to go in as far as when you have very clear water with good visibility. This means, of course, that you shouldn't make penetration dives at night.

2. Linear distances of 40 metres/130 feet.
In open water, your maximum depth shouldn't exceed 40 metres/130 feet. Similarly, your maximum distance from the surface when penetrating a wreck shouldn't exceed the same distance, which means

Limit your wreck penetration to: the edge of the visible light zone, 40 linear metres/130 linear feet from the surface, and one third of your air supply.

that your depth plus your distance from the wreck entry shouldn't exceed 40 metres/130 feet. For example, if you're diving on a wreck 30 metres/100 feet deep, you wouldn't go more than 10 metres/30 feet into the wreck.

3. One third of your air supply.

Overhead environments call for reserving two-thirds of your air for exiting the wreck, and this includes the air you use from the time you leave the surface. For example, if you begin the dive with 200 bar/3000 psi, you would turn around and head for the exit when you reach 133 bar/2000 psi. This essentially means that you use one third in, one third out and one third for reserve.

Overhead environment accident analysis shows that failing to observe this "Rule of Thirds" contributes to accidents. Saving two thirds of your air for exiting gives you more of the most important factor you need to handle a problem inside a wreck: time. You can solve almost any problem given enough time, so you should observe the Rule of Thirds whenever you penetrate a wreck. However, you don't have to surface with all this reserve — just exit the wreck. Once you're outside, you can use your remaining air exploring the wreck's exterior until you reach a conventional open water limit, such as no stop time or appropriate open water reserve.

Wreck Penetration Techniques

Moving through a wreck differs in many ways from swimming through open water. You're traveling through a relatively confined area, and you'll have to return through it, so you need to preserve the visibility by not stirring up silt. You're going along a penetration line or, if you're handling the reel, you're laying and retrieving it. In either case, you'll want to avoid getting tangled or accidentally breaking the line. To complicate matters, you have to do everything by dive light.

You shouldn't find wreck penetration techniques difficult, but they do take some practice. This is why you learn them initially outside the wreck.

Recreational Penetration & Technical Penetration

The technical diving community is a small niche within the dive community, but it can be very visible at times. You may hear about technical divers making extensive penetrations into wrecks, as well as other overhead environments. As a PADI Wreck Diver, you should be familiar with how technical and recreational penetration differ, and why.

Recreational penetration follows the limits you have just learned: Maximum 40 metres/130 feet from the surface and within the light zone. Recreational penetration limits were introduced by the cave diving community in the form of cavern diving. The cave community, which is the oldest and most experienced group in technical diving, recognized that many divers wanted something between open water diving and full fledged technical cave diving. They also recognized that for those few interested in technical cave diving, an intermediate step developed skills to build upon. Recreational wreck penetration limits follow this philosophy, and sprang from cavern diving.

Technical penetrations continue past the light zone and farther than 40 metres/130 feet from the surface. To do this with adequate safety, the diver needs even more extensive equipment than for recreational penetration: multiple redundant air sources, more lights, and other considerations. The training is especially rigorous, because more complicated procedures apply and the margin for error is narrow. **Even when properly equipped and trained, the technical diver faces more risk than a diver who remains within recreational limits.**

Keep in mind that just as the cavern diver interested in cave diving needs additional training beyond the scope of a cavern course, the recreational wreck diver interested in technical wreck penetration requires training and experience beyond the scope of the PADI Wreck Diver program.

Entering the wreck

Ideally, you'll have surveyed the wreck on a previous dive before making your penetration dive, allowing you to descend and swim directly to your entry point. You begin by tying off the penetration line outside.

Look for a sturdy piece of wreckage that's not movable or likely to break, and that doesn't have sharp edges. If possible, thread the line through a hole and tie the line end to itself. Use a knot that releases even after bearing stress, such as a square knot followed by a bowline, a backed up bowline, two half hitches or a clove hitch.

If you're using a standard reel, it's simplest to have a permanent loop in the line end (usually tied with a figure eight knot) large enough to pass the reel through. Pass the line around/through your tie object, then put the reel through the loop to secure the line without a knot. Whether you tie a knot or use a permanent loop, after securing the line, ideally wrap the line another turn around the object.

Wreck penetration begins by securing the penetration line at the entrance.

When ready to enter the wreck, the reel diver goes first. Assuming you're the reel diver, go just inside the entry (remember that it should be large, have no sharp edges and there shouldn't be any risk of closing doors, covers or blockage) and stop. Sweep your light in a circle and look up, around, down and in before proceeding. Look for possible hazards. Let your bubbles hit the ceiling to see if they cause much silt to rain down (if so, abort the penetration).

After you're confident that it's okay to continue,

Knots for Wreck Divers

• **Backed up bowline.** Few knots perform as well as a bowline: it's easy to tie, holds well and unties easily. It doesn't usually jam, even when wet. However, with wet synthetic line, once in a while a bowline may slip. An overhand knot prevents slippage, making this a very secure, yet easy to untie knot.

• **Double bowline.** If you need a loop in the middle of some line, try a double bowline. You can also tie a backup knot on a double bowline.

• **Figure eight knot.** Use this knot when you need a basic knot that's easy to untie, such as if you cut a line and want to keep it from unraveling.

• **Figure eight knot loop.** A figure eight knot loop is considered more secure than a bowline, but it's not nearly as easy to untie, especially after bearing a load. It's a good choice for permanent or semipermanent loops.

• **Two half hitches.** This is your basic "tie a rope to something" general purpose knot.

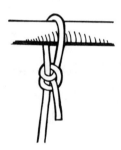

• **Square knot.** Use the square knot with caution. It is a knot that spills easily (gets pulled out of shape), causing slippage. It is designed for use with an even load on both sides of the knot, such as tying a box shut. Its best use in wreck diving is with a more secure knot to provide extra confidence against slippage.

go into the wreck a couple of metres/few feet and wrap the penetration line around a second anchor point. This is in case the outside tie accidentally gets cut or comes free. The line from the primary tie to the secondary tie shouldn't have any slack, but it doesn't need to be excessively tight.

As you continue into the wreck, maintain light tension on the line as it comes off the reel. Slack makes tangling very likely, and can cause some reels to jam. With a beginner's reel and line, you can maintain tension by holding the reel against your side, or by gripping the reel from the center with your thumb and fingers. With a standard reel, use one or two fingers to maintain tension. (Note: If you ever tangle or jam a reel, don't try to untangle it underwater. Abort the penetration and wrap the line around the outside of the reel as you exit. You can clear it later on the surface.)

Wrap the line around nonsharp objects from time to time as necessary to route the line where your buddies can follow it. However, don't make any more wraps than necessary because it makes it harder to follow the line during a siltout. Also, try to keep the line low, since it's harder to follow if it's close to the ceiling.

Moving through the wreck

The proper techniques for moving through a wreck begin with maintaining neutral buoyancy. Once you enter the wreck, stay neutral and stay off the bottom; failure to do this will almost always lead to stirred up silt and reduced visibility.

Inside the wreck, you need to modify your regular kicking. Stay level and use short gentle kicks that don't drop below your body centerline. Use gentler, sculling kicks. The idea is to keep from directing any kicks toward the wreck floor where it will disturb silt.

When practical, gently pull yourself by hand through the wreck. However, to prevent cuts or contact with aquatic life, look closely before you grab anything. If in doubt, don't touch.

Don't use the penetration line to pull yourself along, whether on the way in or on the way out.

Pulling on the line on the way in can spin the reel, causing slack and possible entanglement, jam the reel or pull it out of the reel diver's hand. Pulling on it exiting can fray and break the line, or pull it off a wrap point causing slack.

Inside the wreck, try to do everything slowly and deliberately. You'll find that stirring up some silt is inevitable, but concentrate on keeping it to a minimum. For example, if you find yourself sinking toward the floor, rather than kicking to stay up, use buoyancy control.

Penetration line use

Proper line use minimizes the probability that you or your buddies become entangled in the line as you follow it into and out of the wreck.

As you've already read, the reel diver goes first, maintaining line tension and deploying the line. A recommended maximum of two buddies follow single file, near the line but not holding on to it (except for turns or during emergencies — more on these shortly). If you're not handling the reel, try to swim with the line just below chest level and off to one side, wreck configuration permitting. You should know where to find the line at any time, and be able to reach out and grasp it.

If you need to turn around, either to check on a buddy behind you, to confirm that you're still within the light zone, or to exit the wreck, grasp the line with your hand closest to it. Turn toward the line, holding it clear to avoid snagging and tangling your equipment. Grasp it with your other hand and release with the first to complete the turn.

Upon reaching any limit — 40 linear metres/130 linear feet, edge of light zone, two-thirds air remaining for any diver, etc. — everyone turns to exit the wreck. The last diver now leads, with the reel diver in the rear, taking up the line as you go. Because some silt stirring is unavoidable, don't be surprised if you find less visibility on the way out.

The reel diver is always the first diver in and the last diver out.

Wreck Penetration Emergencies

As long as you observe the penetration limits you've learned, you should have adequate time and

Air, Fuel and Oil Pockets

In some wrecks, you may encounter what appear to be pockets of trapped air left by previous divers. Some of these may be large enough to bring your head out of the water.

Approach all "air pockets" with caution. Some pockets may be trapped fuel, oil or other chemicals from the wreck, which you'll want to avoid. If you find the pocket does contain air, don't breathe it — keep using your regulator. Over time, oxygen dissolves out of trapped air, so that you could lose consciousness trying to breathe it.

As always, when in doubt, keep clear of the pocket completely.

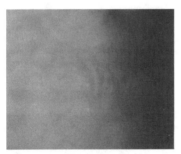

If a siltout occurs, immediately stop, make contact with the line and give the silt a moment to settle out.

resources to handle problems — even potentially severe ones. It's important to stop, breathe, think and then act, just as you would handling any dive problem.

Siltout

A "siltout" occurs when divers kick up the bottom, when bubbles dislodge particles from the wall and ceiling, or when divers don't control their buoyancy and bump into the bottom. If severe, a siltout can reduce visibility to almost zero, making it impossible to see with or without a light.

If silt begins to destroy visibility, immediately make contact with the penetration line by making a loose "O" around it with your hand. Everyone should hold still and give the silt a moment to settle. If it doesn't settle quickly (depends on how coarse the silt is) and visibility is very poor, signal "up" to abort the penetration if there's enough visibility to see your signal. If there's not, everyone should assume the penetration is being aborted.

Turn to the exit, handling the line as you learned, except don't release the line after completing the turn. In siltout conditions, never release the line. Instead, maintain your loose grip as you follow it out. When you reach wrap points, find the line on the other side of the wrap with your other hand before letting go to pass the wrap.

Again, don't pull yourself out by the penetration line. If you're the reel diver and you couldn't see whether all divers made line contact and exited, it's recommended that you leave the reel and follow the line out. This leaves the line in place for the remote possibility that a diver lost line contact and will need to relocate it to exit. You can retrieve the line and reel on a later dive.

Lost or cut penetration line

If you accidentally lose contact with the penetration line, or if it accidentally gets broken or cut, immediately stop and allow any silt to settle. Look for the natural light from the entrance. If you need to turn to do this, do so taking care not to stir up silt.

If you don't see light from the entrance, cover your light (but don't turn it off — bulbs most often

The Command Signal

Inside a wreck, the "thumbs up" signal to surface takes on more authority than in open water. In open water, you might reply with some question signals, such as "how much air do you have?" "let's go over there," then, "surface," etc.

In the overhead environment, the "surface" signal from any diver turns the penetration immediately. Because there's more potential hazard in an overhead environment, the rule is that you don't use any time or air questioning or modifying the command to exit. When the thumb goes up, the divers go out, period.

fail when you turn them off and on) and let your eyes adjust to the dark. After spotting the exit, swim carefully to it. You may also find a map slate helpful in locating the exit if you're tracking your progress on one.

If you're the reel diver and discover one of your buddies has lost the line, it's recommended that you leave the line and reel in place if you must exit before you're sure the diver has found his way out. Again, this leaves the line to help him if he needs it.

Light failure

If your light fails, stop and make loose contact with the line, while using your other hand to retrieve and turn on your backup. If you have only one backup, signal your buddies and abort the penetration. **You shouldn't continue the penetration with only one working light.** Use the backup to allow a safe exit (this is another reason why experienced wreck divers carry three or more lights — they can continue the penetration after a single failure).

If your backup light doesn't work or has been lost, signal your buddy and borrow his, then abort the penetration.

Air supply loss

If you follow the Rule of Thirds, it's highly unlikely you'll run out of air. However, if for some reason you do have an air supply problem, switch to your pony

In an out of air situation, preferably exit the wreck with the donor ahead and the receiver gently holding the donor's tank.

Alternate Air Sources and Hose Length

Since the inside of a wreck can limit how close a donor and a receiver can get, some wreck divers prefer the conventional right-handed second stage on a 1 metre/39 inch or longer hose. A few avid wreck divers use even longer hoses with the slack held against the tank by elastic bands.

Although virtually all alternate air source second stage and alternate inflator regulator configurations work adequately in recreational wreck penetration environments, you may want to consider hose length for improved performance in an out of air situation, especially if you plan to make penetration dives fairly often.

bottle (if you have one) and exit the wreck immediately. Make a normal ascent.

If you don't have a pony bottle, secure your buddy's alternate second stage and immediately exit the wreck. Exit the wreck preferably with the donor ahead, following the line; the receiver gently holds the donor's tank to prevent separation.

If you're the reel diver, whether you're the donor or the receiver it's often simplest to leave the line and reel in place and exit. You can retrieve them on a later dive.

Exercise 7

Wreck Penetration

1. Pieces of equipment for wreck penetration diving include (check all that apply):
   - ☑ a. light and backup light
   - ☑ b. pony bottle
   - ☐ c. lift bag
   - ☑ d. penetration line and reel
   - ☐ e. slate

2. The maximum distance to your point in the wreck is 40 linear metres/130 linear feet from the surface, or the edge of the light zone, whichever is longer.　☐ True　☑ False

3. If you're handling the reel, procedures for entering a wreck include (check all that apply):
   - ☑ a. tying the primary and secondary anchor points
   - ☑ b. looking up and around just inside before proceeding
   - ☐ c. crawling gently along the bottom so your buddy can see past you
   - ☑ d. maintaining neutral buoyancy

4. In case of a siltout, you should gently pull yourself along the penetration line until you exit the wreck.　☐ True　☑ False

How did you do?
1. a, b, d, e.　2. False. The maximum is 40 linear metres/130 linear feet from the surface or the edge of the light zone, whichever is shorter.　3. a, b, d.　4. False. You should follow the penetration line maintaining a loose grip on it, and without pulling on it.

There's no cure for the wreck diving bug – but you can relieve the symptoms by going wreck diving!

A World of Wreck Diving

It's a common cliché that ending a course is "only the beginning," but you often hear it because it's often true; it certainly is with the PADI Wreck Diver course. As you dive on wrecks more and more, chances are your interest in them will grow. Wreck diving can become a passion so that your interest in diving becomes focused on wrecks. You may spend a lot of time researching wrecks, writing about them and talking with fellow wreck divers. If so, chances are the wreck diving bug has bitten you hard. There's no cure, but you can relieve the symptoms a little by going wreck diving.

More likely, you'll find wreck diving one of many diving activities that you enjoy, and one you combine with underwater photography, studying aquatic life and other activities. Still, don't be surprised if, more and more, when offered the choice between a wreck and a nonwreck dive site, you choose the wreck.

A few final thoughts about wreck penetration diving: Much of the PADI Wreck Diver course, this manual and the PADI *Wreck Diving* video deals with penetration, but that's because educationally, there's a lot to cover. However, you may find you have little interest in entering a wreck, either because you don't want to deal with the hassles, you don't think it's worth the added risk, or any number of other reasons. If you don't want to do it, don't. There's plenty of great diving on wrecks without penetration.

If you do have an interest in penetration, do it right. Follow the established limits and always employ the necessary equipment and procedures, no matter how familiar you've become with the wreck inside and out. Accident data show that accidents have happened when trained and experienced overhead environment divers thought they knew the site so well that they didn't apply proper procedures.

Either way, have fun. Wreck diving opens a